How to Thrive in Perilous Times

*Living Beyond
the World System*

By
Happy Caldwell

Harrison House
Tulsa, Oklahoma

12 11 10 09   10 9 8 7 6 5 4 3 2 1

How to Thrive in Perilous Times:
Living Beyond the World System
ISBN 13: 978-1-57794-981-7
ISBN 10: 1-57794-981-1
(Formerly ISBN 0-89274-258-5)
Copyright © 1983, 2009 by Happy Caldwell
Agape Church, Inc.
P. O. Box 22007
Little Rock, Arkansas 72221-2007
www.agape-church.org

Published by Harrison House Publishers
P. O. Box 35035
Tulsa, Oklahoma 74153
www.harrisonhouse.com

Contents

Introduction

Throughout human history, there have always been perilous times that have challenged the faith of men and women everywhere. *Perilous times*, by definition, are dangerous or difficult times. While we cannot prevent perilous times from coming, we can thrive--if we know how.

To *thrive* is to flourish and prosper, even in the midst of perilous times. Isaac, the son of Abraham, is a good Old Testament example of this. He was surrounded by famine. People were packing up their families and their belongings and moving out of town looking for food and work (similar to the Great Depression in this county in the 1920s and 1930s). Yet God spoke to Isaac and told him to stay where he was and that He (God) would be with him and bless him. (Gen. 26:1–6.)

Then Isaac did something that looked and sounded utterly ridiculous. He planted crops, in that land, even though there was famine and drought (perilous times)— and received in the same year a hundredfold harvest. (v. 12.)

Oral Roberts (world-renown evangelist, author, and

educator) shared a story with me one time that was very similar to Isaac's story. It happened to his family when he was a young boy growing up in Oklahoma.

When I was a little boy, my father was a preacher and a farmer. He grew corn, wheat, and a number of other crops in Pontotoc County, Oklahoma. One year a terrible hail storm came through and destroyed the crop— not only our crops, but the crops of every farmer in the area.

Now this was the 1920s. My father had determined that he would never be broke, so he always kept a twenty dollar bill in the "secret compartment" of his wallet, and my mother knew it. After the hail storm, she came out on the front porch of our home and said to my father, "Ellis, get that twenty dollars out of the secret compartment of your wallet, hitch up the wagon, and go into town to Jeter's Feed Store and buy seed; we're going to replant."

My father, in doubt, said, "It's too late in the season to replant..." but he stopped, because he knew my mother was speaking a word from God. So he hitched up the wagon and got me and my brother Vaden, and we drove to Ada, Oklahoma Jeter's Feed Store

Mr. Jeter came out of his store and said, "Can I help you, Brother Roberts?"

He said, "Yes, we've come to buy seed to replant.

My father told us over and over that he felt like a fool trying to replant his farm with twenty dollars. He said, "Mr. Jeter, looked at me as if to say, it's too late... and then something happened. He turned to his workers and said, 'Take Brother Roberts' wagon around behind the feed store and fill it with seed.'"

My father drove that wagon back to our farm and replanted... even though to the natural mind it didn't make sense to replant because it was too late in the season. None of the other farmers in the area replanted, just the Roberts family. And only one farm in that area harvested a crop that year. It was the Roberts farm.

I believe when my mother told my father to replant, she "shifted gears" spiritually. She went from focusing on the seed that was lost to focusing on the new seed, representing what would be harvested.

So as you can see, God can still cause you to thrive in perilous times if you know what to do.

Perhaps the greatest story of thriving in perilous times is the story of Joseph. Joseph was a young man with a dream from God. The dream revealed how God would sustain a nation of people in perilous times. Even though Joseph's brothers were envious and thought to kill him, his dream was from God and was given to accomplish three things: (1) to preserve life; (2) to preserve a posterity in the earth (a remnant); and (3) to save lives by a great deliverance. (Gen. 45:5–7.)

Although Joseph had to overcome many obstacles, the dream eventually became a reality. Most people focus on Joseph's journey rather than the dream. It was the dream (the will of God revealed) that caused him to thrive, not the journey. The journey was not God's idea, it was irrelevant. It was the dream that brought Joseph into Pharaoh's court and made him thrive in perilous times.

When Joseph's brothers realized who he had become, they fell down and worshiped him. And Joseph said unto them, "Fear not: for am I in the place of God? [In other words, am I where God set me?] But as for you, [you] thought evil against me; but God meant it [the dream] unto good, to bring to pass, as it is this day, to save much people alive" (Gen. 50:19–20).

If you are to thrive in perilous times, you have to

first straighten out your thinking. God does not create perilous times to punish you, correct you, get your attention or judge you. Perilous times are usually a result of people's sinfulness, greed, lust, dishonesty, and so on.

God's system operates by faith and love. The world's system operates by fear and greed. God's system began in the Garden of Eden. Man's system began at the Tower of Babel. (Gen. 1:26–29; 11:1–4.)

When you see financial and political chaos, it's usually because of the seeds that have been sown. "Be not deceived; God is not mocked: for whatsoever a man soweth, that shall he also reap. For he that soweth to his flesh [carnal appetites] shall of the flesh reap corruption; but he that soweth to the Spirit shall of the Spirit reap life everlasting" (Gal. 6:7– 8).

The world's system is simply people trying to meet their own needs, without God. In this book, you will discover God's system of how to thrive in perilous times. Four principles will be revealed—two from Jesus and two from the apostle Paul. Perilous times will come and go, but you can thrive in the midst of them.

1

Four Steps to Victorious Living

In Matthew's gospel Jesus told the disciples about things that would come to pass:

Jesus went out, and departed from the temple: and his disciples came to him for to shew him the buildings of the temple.

And Jesus said unto them, See ye not all these things? verily I say unto you, There shall not be left here one stone upon another, that shall not be thrown down.

And as he sat upon the mount of Olives, the disciples came unto him privately, saying, Tell us, when shall these things be? and what shall be the sign of thy coming, and of the end of the world?

Matthew 24:1–3

The disciples asked Jesus three questions here:

(1) when the destruction of the Jewish temple would take place; (2) what the sign of His coming would be; and (3) what would be the sign of the end of the world. His response is divided into three separate areas. Some answers He gave were directed to the Jews of that day, others refer to the Great Tribulation period—neither of which concern us here.

The question we will consider in this book is found in verse 3: "What shall be the sign ... of the end of the world?" Jesus' answer is important to us today because we are living in those last days. Let's see what He had to say about the end times:

Jesus answered and said unto them, Take heed that no man deceive you. For many shall come in my name, saying, I am Christ; and shall deceive many.

And ye shall hear of wars and rumours of wars: see that ye be not troubled: for all these things must come to pass, but the end is not yet.

Matthew 24:4–6

2

There are four specific things we can do to live in perilous times–two are given here by Jesus, the others are found in the writings of the apostle Paul. We will discuss these briefly, then study each in more detail in succeeding chapters.

BE NOT DECEIVED

The first thing Jesus said was: "Take heed that no man deceive you." To take heed is to be careful, to pay attention and concentrate. The word "deceive" is probably the strongest Jesus could use. He was cautioning us about being deceived in these last days. In verse 5 He tells us the deception we are to guard against: "For many shall come in my name, saying, I am Christ; and shall deceive many."

I have received literature that serves as excellent examples of the deception Jesus was talking about. One was a news release addressed to radio and television talk shows, presenting a young man for possible interview. This young man was announcing himself as the Christ, saying he had a message for the world.

Another example was a package of literature delivered to me in the mail. Outside the package were written these words: "Beware! Deliver this material to whom it is addressed. Do not touch it, lest the rays of Karma come upon you and destroy you!" It was from a person who thought himself to be an angel sent from the throne of God to warn me and instruct me to do certain things.

Jesus said that in the last days this would happen. He warned us about being deceived by it: "Take heed that no man deceive you."

BE NOT TROUBLED

In verse 6 Jesus said, "Ye shall hear of wars and rumours of wars: *see that ye be not troubled.*"

In these last days, all kinds of things will come against you to trouble your mind and take away your peace. By listening to these pronouncements of trouble instead of what the Word of God has to say, you can become nervous, anxious, and worried, thinking that things are going from bad to worse.

I don't receive such dire predictions, and neither

should any other believer. Either God's Word works, or it doesn't, and God has said that no weapon formed against you shall prosper. (Isa. 54:17.)

Are you affected when you hear a forecast of threatening weather? That the flu season is on its way? That the stock market is failing? That the economy is getting worse? That unemployment is rising to an all-time high?

Many Christians view bad circumstances as a method God uses to work out some mysterious purpose in their lives. But bad circumstances are Satan's deception to steal from us or destroy our lives. Jesus said, "The thief cometh not but for to steal, and to kill, and to destroy: I am come that they might have life, and…have it more abundantly" (John 10:10). Anxiety, trouble, and fear are not the circumstances of life, but of death. The circumstances of life are health, wealth, and happiness.

If Satan can trouble you and get you to fear, he will have you in his hands. You will become one of his victims.

Don't be a victim of circumstances. Learn to remain

strong and firm in the face of negative circumstances. Take heed that no man deceive you. See that you be not troubled. God hasn't changed places with the devil; He is still on His throne. Jesus is alive, and all is well in the kingdom of God.

THESE THINGS WILL COME

In verse 6 Jesus said, "See that ye be not troubled: for all these things must come to pass ." I emphasize the word "must."

Perilous times are going to come—Jesus said they would—but they don't have to affect your life, not if you know how to deal with them. They may come to steal, kill, and destroy; but they don't have to rob, kill, and destroy you.

People who are confused in their thinking complain, "Why does God let all this happen?" God isn't "letting all this happen." These things are happening because Christians aren't doing anything about them. If we would come together to pray and believe God, the storms, blizzards, droughts, and other such conditions could be averted. We could do what Elijah and Jesus did—stand and rebuke the elements whenever they are harmful to humanity.

In 2 Timothy 3:1 the apostle Paul wrote, "This know also, that in the last days perilous times shall come." He was warning Timothy about the same things Jesus said would come to pass.

Perilous times *are* coming; but they are not from God and should not be received by God's people.

As Christians we can live above the circumstances— the layoffs and financial problems, the sickness and disease that plague so many people today.

CONTINUE IN THE THINGS YOU HAVE LEARNED

In 2 Timothy 3:14 the apostle Paul tells us what to do to live in perilous times: "But *continue thou in the things which thou hast learned* and hast been assured of, knowing of whom thou hast learned them."

Jesus stood in the temple on the Sabbath day and

read these words from the book of Isaiah:

> The Spirit of the Lord is upon me, because he hath anointed me to preach the gospel [good news] to the poor; he hath sent me to heal the brokenhearted, to preach deliverance to the captives, and recovering of sight to the blind, to set at liberty them that are bruised, to preach the acceptable year of the Lord.
>
> *Luke 4:18,19*

This is what Jesus came to do—to preach good news, to heal, to deliver, to set people free—and He has not changed. "Jesus Christ [is] the same yesterday, and to day, and for ever" (Heb. 13:8).

The church today should be teaching God's people how to live in victory over trials and tribulations. Then we should be acting on what we learn. We are responsible for the things we learn in the Word of God. As Paul said, "Continue thou in the things which thou hast learned."

KNOW THE WORD

In 2 Timothy 3:15 we find the second of Paul's instructions on how to live in perilous times: "And that from a child *thou hast known the holy scriptures, which are able to make thee wise* unto salvation through faith which is in Christ Jesus."

Think a moment about all the great men of God, Old Testament and New, who had to rely on God's wisdom. Think of the prophet Elijah. During a time of famine in Israel, God sent ravens every day to bring Elijah bread and meat. (1 Kings 17.) When the brook dried up and there was no water, God sent him to the home of a widow and provided food for them. Though there was a famine going on, God took care of His own.

There are many "famines" in the earth today—unemployment, poverty, starvation, sickness. But perhaps the most serious famine concerns the Word of God. People are especially lacking in the Word. They are starving to death spiritually. Paul said simply, "Know the Scriptures and they will make you wise."

That wisdom, a godly wisdom, will enable you to live victoriously in these perilous times.

Here are the four steps to victorious living:

1. Be not deceived.

2. Be not troubled.

3. Continue in the things you have learned.

4. Know the Word.

Now let's look at each step in more detail.

2

Be Not Deceived

Take heed that no man deceive you.
Matthew 24:4

Satan's attack on the saints of God has reached an all-time high. He is engaged in an all-out war against the body of Christ—a war of deception. Never before in man's history has the devil tried so hard to deceive. Deception is his only real weapon, the only way he can operate. Let me show you what I mean.

THE ENEMY COMES IN *LIKE* A FLOOD

The last part of Isaiah 59:19 reads: "When the enemy shall come in like a flood, the Spirit of the Lord shall lift up a standard against him."

The word *flood* in the Bible is used most always in reference to God, to His omnipotence, and His all-consuming power.

For instance, when God covered the earth with a flood, He said, "I will put the rainbow in the clouds as a sign unto man that never again will I destroy the earth with a flood." (Gen. 9:12–17.) That was a flood of destruction and devastation to cleanse the earth of sin. God saved only Noah and his family because Noah had found grace in God's eyes.

In Malachi 3:10 God says: "Bring ye all the tithes into the storehouse, that there may be meat in mine house, and prove me now herewith, saith the Lord of hosts, if I will not open you the *windows* of heaven, and pour you out a blessing, that there shall not be room enough to receive it." The word translated "windows" actually means "sluice," which is a channel of water regulated by a floodgate.[1] So God is speaking here of a flood of blessings.

Isaiah 59:19—"When the enemy shall come in like

[1] *Blue Letter Bible, "Dictionary and Word Search for 'arubbah' (Strong's 699)," copyright © 1996-2009, available at http:// www.blueletterbible.org/lang/ lexicon/lexicon.cfm?Strongs=H699&t=KJV, S.V. "windows," Malachi 3:10.*

a flood…"—tells us that Satan is not a flood; he just comes in like one. He tries to give the appearance of a flood and deceive us into thinking he is one.

Another Scripture verse that will help us understand this is 1 Peter 5:8, which says, "Be sober, be vigilant; because your adversary the devil, as a roaring lion, walketh about, seeking whom he may devour." Satan is walking around, roaring loudly, trying to make people think he is a fierce lion. But he is not a lion, he is only masquerading as one. All he can do is roar, to frighten and deceive people. He can't really harm us because Jesus has given us power over him.

James 4:7 says, "Resist the devil, and he will flee from you." Can you resist a flood? No. A flood is irresistible, uncontainable. It will overwhelm all in its path. Yet James says resist the devil and he will flee from us. If Satan were really a flood, we would be unable to resist him, to stop or contain him. He would be able to run roughshod over all the world, over all the Church of Jesus Christ, and we could do nothing about it.

Satan is not a flood, though he tries hard to make us think he is. The only way he can cause destruction in our lives is by convincing us that he is a flood so we will give place to him.

Satan is trying to deceive the church, but we don't have to succumb to his deception. All the calamity and destruction happening in the church would cease if the body of Christ would just stand up and resist the devil. He would have to flee from us. God's Word says so: "Take heed that no man deceive you" (Matt. 24:4).

THE STANDARD OF GOD

"When the enemy shall come in like a flood, the Spirit of the Lord shall lift up a standard against him" (Isa. 59:19). To lift up a standard against an enemy means to put him to flight, to chase him away. God has promised that when Satan comes against us—trying to deceive us, pretending to be a flood to overwhelm us—if we will stand firm against him, God will raise up a standard against him and put him to flight.

The problem has been that the church has not always stood firm against the enemy. Many times when they heard Satan's roar and saw him advance like a floodtide, they were deceived. They acted out of fear, allowing themselves to be defeated.

THE PRICE OF IGNORANCE

Paul wrote about just such times as these in his second letter to Timothy:

> I charge thee therefore before God, and the Lord Jesus Christ, who shall judge the quick and the dead at his appearing and his kingdom; Preach the word; be instant [or diligent] in season, out of season; reprove, rebuke, exhort with all longsuffering and doctrine. For the time will come when they [the Christians] will not endure sound doctrine; but after their own lusts [desires] shall they heap to themselves teachers, having itching ears; and they shall turn away their ears from the truth, and shall be turned unto fables [fiction].
>
> *2 Timothy 4:1–4*

Satan's biggest ploy against the church today is deception. He has sent deceiving spirits to lead God's people to destruction. Ignorance of Satan and his devices is deception. Many Christians have no idea of what is happening to them or why.

Paul is saying to Timothy in this passage: "There is coming a time when the Christians will not endure sound doctrine; but after their own lusts and desires, they will heap to themselves teachers to tell them everything their itching ears want to hear."

Some people don't want to hear the whole gospel, just "the good stuff." "Never mind about holiness or living the clean life, tell me about prosperity, about making money and getting rich!" Some people have departed from the pure Gospel of Jesus Christ and have given themselves over to their own lust and greed.

Satan's great deception is to lead people away from the truth and get them listening to fables—things that are not biblical.

TEST THE SPIRITS

In *1 John 4:1–4*, we are warned:

Beloved, believe not every spirit, but try the spirits whether they are of God: because many false prophets are gone out into the world. Hereby know ye the Spirit of God: Every spirit that confesseth that Jesus Christ is come in the flesh is of God: And every spirit that confesseth not that Jesus Christ is come in the flesh is not of God: and this is that spirit of antichrist, whereof ye have heard that it should come; and even now already is it in the world. Ye are of God, little children, and have overcome them: because greater is he that is in you, than he that is in the world.

Don't believe every spirit, but try the spirits—test and prove them to see whether they are of God.

Jesus said that a tree is known by its fruit. (Matt. 12:33.) He also said, "Not every one that saith unto me, Lord, Lord, shall enter into the kingdom of heaven; but he that doeth the will of my Father which is in heaven"

(Matt. 7:21). To judge or test the spirits you must do as Paul said: "Examine my life. Look at my purpose, my love. Consider the fruit that is coming from my life."

SATAN IS A *LIAR*

Satan has been deceiving people since the Garden of Eden. Look at what happened then:

> Now the serpent was more subtle than any beast of the field which the Lord God had made. And he said unto the woman, Yea, hath God said, Ye shall not eat of every tree of the garden? And the woman said unto the serpent, We may eat of the fruit of the trees of the garden: but of the fruit of the tree which is in the midst of the garden, God hath said, Ye shall not eat of it, neither shall ye touch it, lest ye die. And the serpent said unto the woman, Ye shall not surely die: for God doth know that in the day ye eat thereof, then your eyes shall be opened, and ye shall be as gods, knowing good and evil.
>
> *Genesis 3:1–5*

The first step in Satan's deception was an outright lie. He told Eve, *"Ye shall not surely die"*—a direct contradiction of what God had told Adam in *Genesis 2:16–17:*

> And the Lord God commanded the man, saying, Of every tree of the garden thou mayest freely eat: But of the tree of the knowledge of good and evil, thou shalt not eat of it: for in the day that thou eatest thereof thou shalt surely die.

Satan's second step in his deception was to cast doubt on God's motives and character. In essence, he told Eve, "God doesn't want you to eat of the fruit. He knows that if you do, your eyes will be opened and you'll be as gods." This was his second lie. Adam and Eve didn't have to eat that fruit to be as gods; they were already gods, made in the image and likeness of Almighty God. (Gen. 1:26.) They already had dominion over the earth and were exactly what Satan was trying to tell them they would become.

The serpent told Eve that she and Adam could become *like* God if they would be disobedient *to* God. What a deception! You can never become more like God by being dishonest to Him.

That was Satan's ploy to deceive Adam and Eve into doing what God had expressly told them not to do. *Disobedience to God is always a deception, and it is always from the devil.*

As a result of that deception, sin entered the heart of mankind. The Bible says that the woman was deceived in the transgression, but the man was not; he willfully disobeyed God. (1 Tim. 2:14.) It was Adam's duty to see that the garden was kept secure, but he allowed Satan to intrude and spread lies in his domain. He allowed his wife to be deceived by the devil; then he willfully joined her in that disobedience.

Adam partook of the fruit consciously when he should have exercised his rightful authority.

He should have said, "No, Eve, we're not going to eat of that fruit. God told us not to. We're going to obey

God, not the serpent!"

Then he should have turned to that serpent and said, "I hold dominion over this garden, and you have no right to be here, so get out!"

Had he stood firm and ordered the devil out of the garden, no deception would have taken place. There would have been none of the suffering and torment that sin brings.

You can see what happens as a result of deception. Satan is a deceiver, a destroyer.

FOUR DIVISIONS OF SATAN'S KINGDOM

Finally, my brethren, be strong in the Lord, and in the power of his might. Put on the whole armour of God, that ye may be able to stand against the wiles of the devil. For we wrestle not against flesh and blood, but against principalities, against powers, against the rulers of the darkness of this world, against spiritual wickedness in high places.

Ephesians 6:10–12

In this passage we see the four divisions in Satan's kingdom.

First are the *principalities*, the demonic forces which deal with nations and governments. The reason there is so much deception in high-ranking offices around the world today is due to these principalities. They are assigned to deceive the people into thinking there is no God, that the Bible is not true, that they don't need Christianity.

Second are the *powers*. These spirits have authority open to them in all areas. When an ungodly man gives himself over to an evil spirit and is manipulated by that spirit, he has opened himself up to be controlled by one of these powers.

Third are the *rulers*, the governors of spiritual darkness who are blinding the world at large and keeping people from being saved. Paul wrote: "The god of this world hath blinded the minds of them which believe not, lest the light of the glorious gospel of Christ, who is the image of God, should shine unto them" (2 Cor. 4:4).

Fourth are the *wicked spirits*. These are the working forces, the evil spirits who carry out the *assignments* of the principalities, powers, and rulers. They are the forces sent to propagate and spread deceiving doctrines in the church.

DECEIVING DOCTRINES

In 2 Timothy 4:1–4, Paul said that in the last days people will no longer endure sound doctrine, but will turn their ears from the truth and listen instead to fables, fiction, and deceiving doctrines.

Let's look for a moment at these deceiving doctrines. If you are not to be deceived, you must be able to recognize a deceiving doctrine when you hear one. Here are four characteristics of deceiving doctrines:

1. Deceiving doctrines weaken the authority of the Scriptures.

Any doctrine which teaches that it is not God's will to be healed, blessed, prospered, and delivered is a deceiving doctrine. No matter how sincere and well-meaning they may be, the people teaching such things are propagating a deceiving doctrine, one that weakens the authority of the Scriptures. The Scriptures say, "Beloved, I wish above all things that thou mayest prosper and be in health, even as thy soul prospereth" (3 John 2).

In Mark 1:40–45 a leper who came to Jesus for healing said, "Master, if You will, You can heal me." Jesus' reply was simple. He reached out, touched the leper, and said, "I will; be thou clean" (v. 41). That is God's will for the sick. Any teaching contrary to that is a deceiving doctrine.

Romans 12:2 tells us: "Be not conformed to this world: but be ye transformed by the renewing of your mind, that ye may prove what is that good, and acceptable, and perfect, will of God." The words "good," " acceptable," and "perfect" are adjectives describing God's will for you. Anyone who says otherwise is deceiving you.

First Corinthians 10:13 makes a profound

statement: "There hath no temptation taken you but such as is common to man: but God is faithful, who will not suffer you to be tempted above that ye are able; but will with the temptation also make a way to escape, that ye may be able to bear [deal with] it." We usually hear this verse quoted another way: "God will not put any more on you than you can bear." That is not what it says.

The *New American Standard Bible* puts it into more modern English: "God…will not *allow* you to be tempted beyond what you are able." The Bible does not say that God puts temptation on *you*. " Let no man say when he is tempted, I am tempted of God: for God cannot be tempted with evil, neither tempteth he any man" (James 1:13). But God is faithful to provide you a way to escape from it.

To say that God puts temptation on people is a deceiving doctrine. It weakens the authority of the Scriptures. Some ministers stand in their pulpits every Sunday morning and preach deceiving doctrines, not because they want to deceive God's people, but because they themselves are deceived.

2. Deceiving doctrines distort the teaching of the Scriptures.

Believers today, people seeking God and desiring to do His will, are not immune to deceiving doctrines. One particular distortion of the Scriptures is based on a portion of Romans 4:17 that says, "God…quickeneth the dead, and calleth those things which be not as though they were."

Some people have perverted this verse. They are calling things which be as though they were not. That is deception, and it is dangerous.

Suppose you have sickness in your body. It would be wrong to deny the existence of that sickness and say, "I'm not sick. I don't feel pain. There is no sickness or disease in my body."

God doesn't call things which be as though they were not; He calls those things which be not as though they were. There is a difference. Your goal or objective is not negative; it is positive—to be well, to be whole, to live in divine health.

God's Word declares what you are in Christ Jesus: "By His stripes I am healed." "My God meets all my needs." These are scriptural confessions. They are positive, not negative. They affirm what is, according to the Word of God. They call those things which be not as though they were. "Let the redeemed of the Lord say so" (Ps. 107:2). "Let the weak say, I am strong" (Joel 3:10).

When you make a positive confession of what God's Word says about you and your situation, you are calling those things into existence. Like God, you are speaking of things that are not as though they were. To deny the existence of sickness and poverty is to deny fact. Those things do exist. If you deny them, you have left the truth and have stepped into a deceiving doctrine.

You don't deny the existence of sickness and disease; you deny its right to exist in your body! The only way you can change circumstances is to do what God told Abraham to do— call those things that are not as though they were.

Suppose someone stole your car during the night. It would be ridiculous for you to stand in your driveway the next morning and say, "My car is not gone! My car is not gone!" But if you stand there and say, "No weapon formed against me shall prosper," you will be on firm scriptural ground. (See Isa. 54:17.)

To "confess" that your car is not gone is self-delusion. To confess in faith that no weapon of the enemy shall prosper against you is biblical, and it will produce results.

Proverbs 6:30–31 says that if a thief is caught stealing, "he shall restore sevenfold." On the authority of that scripture, you can make the thief repay you seven times the value of that which was stolen from you.

You can call those things that be not as though they were. But you cannot do the opposite. To do so would be distorting the Scriptures.

3. Deceiving doctrines add to the Scriptures the thoughts of men.

One deceiving doctrine that wicked spirits have

perpetrated on the church is praying "if it be Thy will."

Tacking "if it be Thy will" onto a prayer robs it of its power, yet people do it all the time. They stand in church and pray, "Lord, bless us, if it be Thy will." They pray over a sick person, "Lord, heal this dear person, if it be Thy will."

These are honest, sincere Christians who mean no harm. They just don't realize that they have allowed a deceiving doctrine to control their thinking.

4. Deceiving doctrines completely put aside the Scriptures.

Satan sends problems to try to convince Christians that God's Word doesn't work. His plan is to deceive people into turning away from God's Word and completely setting aside the Scriptures.

I have seen people come to church, get saved, and start living a Christian life. But when some problem came up, they ran the other way. Such people are doing precisely what Satan wants them to do. Don't run *away* from the Word of God when you have problems; run *to* it!

SATAN'S BATTLEGROUND

All deception starts in the mind. The mind is Satan's battleground. If the devil can deceive your mind, he can eventually control you—spirit, mind, and body.

In *Romans 12:1–2*, Paul gives some instruction about successful Christian living:

> I beseech you therefore, brethren, by the mercies of God, that ye present your bodies a living sacrifice, holy, acceptable unto God, which is your reasonable service.

You are to *present* your body. Don't wait for God to take it; present it to Him by a conscious act of your will. The Christian life is not a passive existence. You must take action if you expect to see results. This is your reasonable spiritual service.

> And be not conformed to this world: but be ye transformed by the renewing of your mind, that ye may prove what is that good, and acceptable, and perfect, will of God.

If you are to prove the perfect will of God in your life, you must stand against the ways of the world and be transformed! There is only one way that can happen: renew your mind with the Word of God. To successfully resist deception from Satan and his demons, you must know the truth. To resist sickness, poverty, or any of Satan's other attacks, you must know the truth. To do battle with a deceiving, lying spirit from the devil, you have only one weapon—the truth of God's Word. Always remember that. Whenever you meet a deception, hit it head-on with the truth. The truth always wins out.

Remember too that your resistance to deception takes place in the mind. The truth comes from your spirit, but the battle takes place in your mind. Don't be conformed to this world, but be transformed by the *renewing* of your mind.

SATAN'S WEAPONRY

Is Satan more powerful than you? Not if you are a New Testament believer. According to the apostle

John, "Greater is he that is in you, than he that is in the world" (1 John 4:4). Jesus said, "Behold, I give unto you power to tread on serpents and scorpions, and over all the power of the enemy: and nothing shall by any means hurt you" (Luke 10:19). Satan is no match for God or for you. God's Word says so! But you need to know what your power is. For centuries, Satan has been tromping over the church of Jesus Christ only because we have not fully understood our authority.

As we have read in 1 Peter 5:8, "Your adversary the devil, as a roaring lion, walketh about, seeking whom he may devour." Satan is looking for someone to devour. Can he devour you? Any Christian who knows his authority would declare most emphatically, "No, Satan can't devour me!" and he would be right—he can't! But sometimes he does. He has in the past: if you've ever let down your guard, you've opened yourself to his maneuvers.

When we Christians let down our defenses, we allow the devil to break through and devour us. The way he gets us to let down our guard is with his "big gun," his most effective weapon: deception. He tricks us by distorting God's Word—adding to it or subtracting from it—and plants seeds of doubt about the Word in our minds.

Here is an example of how the devil whispers deception to believers: "I know you're a dedicated Christian, but all Christians don't get healed. It may not be God's will for you to be healed. This sickness may be God's test. He may want you to suffer in order to learn patience and humility. He may be putting you through this situation to strengthen you and draw you closer to Him, teaching you to be more dependent upon Him. After all, the Bible says, 'My grace is sufficient for thee.' Don't resist this disease. God is working out His divine will in it. Remember, 'All things work together for good.' Let God have His way with you." (See 2 Cor. 12:9; Rom. 8:28.)

The devil is distorting the Scriptures and raising doubts about them in this person's mind. He is deceiving this person into thinking he is being humble, submissive, and obedient to *God*; while, in reality, he is being humble, submissive, and obedient to the prince of this world—Satan!

RESIST THE DEVIL

Many times Christians are too passive about their Christianity. They may have Scripture verses tacked on the refrigerator and confession cards in their Bibles. They may listen to their CD's, read their books, and watch their favorite preacher on television. But the first time a problem comes and they are persecuted for righteousness' sake, they fold up like an accordion.

Satan is trying to find out what believers are made of. When he comes against some Christians with pressures, persecutions, and afflictions, their first reaction is: "Dear Lord, I didn't think I was supposed to have any trouble. I have my CD's, my books, signs on my refrigerator, and a bumper sticker on my car. I go to church, listen to my radio preacher, and watch Brother Doodad on TV. Why am I having these trials? I didn't think good Christians had problems."

When Christians start giving ear to the Word of God, Satan will try everything he can to get that Word out of them, to convince them that it doesn't work. We must be prepared for his attacks.

None of these things—CDs, DVDs, podcasts, books, radio and television sermons (as good as they may be)—can fully prepare a person to stand against Satan. They are not substitutes for God's Word. To successfully stand against Satan's onslaughts, a believer must renew his mind and build up his spirit man through prayer, Bible study, and meditation in God's Word.

When Satan comes to deceive us, we should follow the instruction in 1 Peter 5:9. It says we are to resist him "steadfast [firmly] in the faith." Say, "No, Satan, you're not going to devour me! I know God's Word." Then give him a dose of that Word.

KNOW THE TRUTH

Then said Jesus to those Jews which believed on him, If ye continue in my word, then are ye my disciples indeed; And ye shall know the truth, and the truth shall make you free.

John 8:31,32

Truth alone will not make anybody free. It is *knowledge* of the truth that sets people free. Truth is available in the world, but many people are still in bondage because they don't know that truth. They may have heard the gospel, but it takes more than just hearing the Word. It must get down into their hearts. Many people hear with their ears, but not with their hearts.

You can know *about* God's Word; but if you don't *know* the Word, Satan will defeat you with deception. To resist that deception, you must *know* the truth. "Ye shall know the truth and the truth shall make you free." You have to know that God wants you well, prosperous, and living the abundant life. You learn that by reading and studying God's Word.

But it is not enough to *know* the truth; you must do something with it. James 2:17 tells us, "Faith, if it hath not works, is dead, being alone." Like faith, knowledge of the truth will not suffice; it will not set you free. You have to add action to your faith, to your knowledge of the truth. James 4:7 says, "Submit yourselves therefore to God. *Resist the devil*, and he will flee from you." To *resist* means to oppose with force.

It sometimes seems as if we read the word "resist" in that verse as *ignore*. "Submit yourselves therefore to God. *Ignore* the devil, and he will flee from you." But he won't! You have to *resist* him, to come against him with opposing force. That opposing force is the Word of God.

You resist Satan's main weapon—deception—with your own main weapon—the truth of God's Word.

SYMPTOMS OF DECEPTION

You learn to recognize deception the way you recognize disease—by its symptoms, its identifying characteristics or danger signs. There are three main symptoms of deception.

1. Double-mindedness

James 1:8 tells us, "A double minded man is

unstable in all his ways." To be double-minded means to be unsteady, unsure, to rock back and forth like a seesaw, to be in faith one minute and in doubt the next.

"I believe it's God's will that I be healed, but I really feel bad."

"I know God will supply my needs, but I'm going bankrupt."

If this describes you, then you are double-minded. You must know the truth of God's Word; then resist the devil, standing against him with all the truth you know. And you must not waver, "For he that wavereth is like a wave of the sea driven with the wind and tossed" (v. 6).

2. Mental Lethargy

Mental lethargy is easily defined and easily recognized. It is simply mental laziness.

"I don't really feel like studying the Bible or praying. I think I'll just watch television. "

That kind of mental lethargy opens a person to deception. As Satan is walking about, seeking whom he may devour, he sees a man sitting in his easy chair, watching TV. Before long, this guy gets laid off at the factory. His wife threatens to leave him. He learns that his kids are on drugs and in trouble at school. He has problems!

This man has not developed his spiritual muscles. He has allowed mental lethargy to set in. When he finds himself under attack from Satan on all sides, he doesn't know what to do about it. He let it come in on him by putting down his guard, and Satan took advantage of it.

3. Apathy

Apathy could also be called inertia, inactivity, or passivity—the "ho-hum" kind of attitude in people who say: "Everything is in God's hands. If He wants me to prosper, He'll prosper me. If He wants me to be well, He'll heal me. Whatever will be, will be. I'll just wait until tomorrow and see what happens. Tomorrow is another day." Any person who talks this way is deceived.

Apathy is really a counterfeit surrender and false sense of submission to God. People who are passive have been deceived into thinking that God will do everything for them. That person is an open target for Satan.

STAND FIRM

Satan is a liar, and he will deceive you if you let him. Don't listen to him. Don't be double-minded, mentally lethargic, or apathetic to the things of God. Don't let anyone tell you it is God's will for you to suffer, to be a failure, to be sick, in poverty, or in pain. Learn God's will for your life. Study His Word. Learn the truth. Then take that truth and use it to resist the devil; he will flee from you.

You can live victoriously in perilous times. But to do so, you must take heed that no man deceive you. (Matt. 24:4.)

3

Be Not Troubled

See that ye be not troubled.

Matthew 24:6

To better understand this commandment, let's see what else Jesus had to say about our preparation for the end times. In *Luke 21:34* He said:

Take heed to yourselves, lest at any time your hearts be overcharged with surfeiting, and drunkenness, and cares of this life, and so that day come upon you unawares.

Here Jesus groups in the same category overeating (surfeiting), drunkenness, and the cares of this life. All are dangerous. People usually overeat because of insecurity, anxiety, and worry. They overeat to compensate for some care in their lives. They are nervous and anxious; they feel unloved and insecure. So they eat ... and eat ... and eat. Jesus said our hearts can be overcharged with overeating just as with drunkenness.

People may give many reasons for why they drink, but there is really only one reason. No matter what they try to tell you (and themselves!), people don't drink alcohol because it tastes good, or because they enjoy it, or because it is so sophisticated. They drink to escape reality. Then they become addicted to it. Alcohol is as addictive as any other drug.

People who drink alcohol and overeat are seeking false courage; they want to dull their senses and escape from reality.

There are other ways people have to escape the cares of this life. They engage in illicit sex, adultery, and fornication. They take pills. They watch pornographic movies. Some watch twenty hours of television a day. Others daydream. Others just go to sleep. They crawl into bed, pull the covers up to their chin, assume the prenatal position, and return to their mother's womb in their mind. People use all kinds of ways to escape facing the real world.

Jesus warned us to be careful about the cares and concerns of this life. He told us plainly, "See that ye be not troubled."

SEE TO IT

You see to it that you be not troubled. This is *your* responsibility.

You may say, "But, Brother Caldwell, I can't help being troubled." Yes, you can. Otherwise, Jesus would not have told you to do so. This, however, will require more of you than just attending church once on Sunday. You will have to spend time with God and in His Word.

Some born-again, Bible-toting Christians think they can wait until they get sick or are in dire need of money before they start appropriating the proper scriptures. They wait until the great hour of need arises or some catastrophe strikes and expect the principles of faith to work in them like they worked in Jesus. They won't!

The time to handle needs, problems, and catastrophes is before they happen. See to the Word.

See that you are not troubled.

Psalm 112 describes the blessedness of the person who trusts in the Lord and is firmly grounded in His Word:

> Blessed is the man that feareth the Lord, that delighteth greatly in his commandments. He shall not be afraid of evil tidings: his heart is fixed, trusting in the Lord. His heart is established, he shall not be afraid, until he sees his desire upon his enemies.
>
> *Psalm 112:1,7,8*

You thrive in perilous times by being prepared for them beforehand. When they come, you won't be affected because you are established in God's Word—your heart is full of the Word and your mind is renewed.

Like a computer, your mind should be programmed with God's Word.

When the computer in our office has been programmed with the proper information, it refuses to receive wrong information and flashes a warning signal: "Argument. Argument."

This is how Christians ought to be—programmed to receive only correct information.

You may ask, "How can I know what is true?" Saturate yourself with God's Word and you will be properly programmed. Then you will be able to distinguish truth from deception.

CARES OF THIS WORLD

In the fourth chapter of Mark, Jesus shared a parable which relates to this subject of the Word and deception. His disciples came to Him later and asked what He meant. Here is part of what He told them:

> These are they which are sown among thorns; such as hear the word, And the cares of this world, and the deceitfulness of riches, and the lusts of other things entering in, choke the word, and it becometh unfruitful.
>
> *Mark 4:18,19*

Even dedicated Christians can allow things to come in and choke the Word until it becomes unfruitful in their lives.

When Jesus used the term "cares of this world," He meant the burdens of this world. To one person that burden might be making a living. To him getting up in the morning, driving to work, and coming home at night, five days a week, is a burden. He could let that burden enter in and choke the Word.

There is a difference between care and responsibility. A person must assume certain responsibilities to be a mature, reliable, and capable human being. He must accept the responsibility that is placed upon him, but not the care of it. A person can fulfill a responsibility and do a job properly without letting the care of the job affect him.

GODLY CONTENTMENT

Jesus said in these last days we would have to live in the midst of turmoil and trouble. But we can be overcomers and live above the problems. One way is by being content.

In 1 Timothy 6, Paul shared a tremendous secret about contentment. He was writing to Timothy, his son in the faith, instructing him to continue the work of the gospel. Paul was warning Timothy against false apostles, false prophets, and other things that were to take place in the days ahead. His advice and counsel was:

> Godliness with contentment is great gain. For we brought nothing into this world, and it is certain we can carry nothing out.
>
> *1 Timothy 6:6,7*

Most denominational traditionalists interpret this passage as saying: "We had nothing when we came into this world, and we won't take anything with us when we leave. Therefore, we are not supposed to have anything while we are in this world."

But God is not saying we are to have nothing; He is telling us to be happy and content with what we do have.

> And having food and raiment let us be therewith content. But they that will be [desire to be] rich fall into temptation and a snare, and into many foolish and hurtful lusts, which drown men in destruction and perdition. For

the love of money is the root of all evil: which
while some coveted after, they have erred from
the faith, and pierced themselves through with
many sorrows. But thou, O man of God, flee
these things [(what things? The love of money,
which is the root of all evil]; and follow after
righteousness, godliness, faith, love, patience,
meekness. Fight the good fight of faith, lay
hold on eternal life.

1 Timothy 6:8–12

In verse 6 Paul said that godliness with contentment
is great gain; then he explained how to be content and
avoid being caught up in the things that will rob us of
contentment.

CONTENTMENT VS. SATISFACTION

There is a difference between contentment and
satisfaction. Don't confuse them. *Contentment* is
uncomplaining acknowledgement of one's state or
position. To *satisfy* is to gratify one's desires or wants
of a particular moment.

Let me give you an example. If you were hungry, you could stuff yourself with all kinds of food. You would be "satisfied" in the sense that you have fulfilled your hunger. You have gratified your desire or want at the time, but that does not mean you are content.

I have seen people stuff themselves with food and complain about every morsel they put in their mouths. Though they "satisfied" their hunger, they were never content.

Contentment is an uncomplaining acknowledgement of one's state. Paul told Timothy, "Learn to be content, and you won't be troubled."

LEARN TO BE CONTENT

If anyone knew how to be content, it was Paul. (Read 2 Corinthians 11 and see the things he suffered for the sake of the gospel—hunger, thirst, cold, beatings, imprisonment, ship¬wreck, persecution, stoning.) Surely if anyone could tell us how to live contentedly and victoriously in the midst of perilous times, it would be the apostle Paul. Here is what he wrote to the church in Philippi about godly contentment:

> I rejoiced in the Lord greatly, that now at the last your care of me hath flourished again; wherein ye were also careful, but ye lacked opportunity. Not that I speak in respect of want: for I have learned, in whatsoever state I am, therewith to be content.
>
> *Philippians 4:10,11*

Paul *learned* how to be content.

Be careful when you read this passage. Many people have misunderstood it and said, "I'll just sit here in my need and wait for God to turn on the glory spout. I'm satisfied to be without and have nothing because, like Paul, whatever state I'm in, I'm content." Paul was not teaching us to passively accept whatever comes without resisting and bear up under anything the devil might care to put on us.

You can take the Word of God and change those bad circumstances in your life. But you can never change them by being satisfied. If you are troubled, the circumstances will change you. But if you are content, you can be victorious over those circumstances.

To gain means to make progress, to profit, to increase. If you are content, you can profit from those circumstances, not just bear up under them. Contentment does not mean the situation will never change; it simply means you are acknowledging it without complaint. You will never change any circumstance by complaining. You change things by applying the Word of God.

> I have learned, in whatsoever state I am, therewith to be content. I know both how to be abased, and I know how to abound: every where and in all things I am instructed both to be full and to be hungry, both to abound and to suffer need. I can do all things through Christ which strengtheneth me.
>
> *Philippians 4:11–13*

Paul did not say he would rather be abased and made low, or that he would rather abound. He said, "I know how to do both."

Contentment does not mean accepting whatever circumstances come. It means a peace of mind and heart that comes from knowing God can and will deliver you out of those circumstances.

Some people are never content, but always complaining. Contentment is great gain. You have to *learn* to be content.

Paul is not saying he had no problems, because he did, or that he was happy with those problems, because he wasn't. But he refused to worry, fret, or become troubled about his circumstances, so he could be content—*in* them, not *with* them.

WITHOUT COVETOUSNESS

In Hebrews 13:5 we read: "Let your conversation [general behavior] be without covetousness; and *be content with such things as ye have*: for he [God] hath said, I will never leave thee, nor forsake thee."

Being content means letting your conversation (general behavior) be without covetousness. Don't get troubled, anxious, and nervous trying to be something you are not. Learn to be happy about yourself. Be content with yourself first. Then learn to be content with your mate, your children, your possessions, your job.

That does not mean you should accept a lower standard of living. Always have higher goals and aspirations. The Bible does not say you are never to desire anything better than you have now. Psalm 37:4 says, "Delight thyself also in the Lord; and he shall give thee the desires of thine heart." Put God's desires before your own; and as He has promised, He will give you the desires of your heart. But if you expect to delight yourself in God, you will have to be content (happy) with such things as you have. No one is going to get anything better from God until he learns to be content with what he already has.

God also tells us in Hebrews 13:5, "I will never leave thee nor forsake thee." Always remember, the Lord is your helper. He will never leave you nor forsake you. With God on your side, you *can thrive* in perilous times. "See that ye be not troubled" (Matt. 24:6).

4

Continue in the Things You Have Learned

But thou has fully known my doctrine, manner of life, purpose, faith, long-suffering, charity, patience, persecutions, afflictions, which came unto me at Antioch, at Iconium, at Lystra; what persecutions I endured: but out of them all the Lord delivered me. Yea, and all that will live godly in Christ Jesus shall suffer persecution. But evil men and seducers shall wax worse and worse, deceiving, and being deceived. But continue thou in the things which thou has learned and hast been assured of, knowing of whom thou hast learned them; And that from a child thou hast known the holy scriptures, which are able to make thee wise unto salvation through faith which is in Christ Jesus.

2 Timothy 3:10–15

In this passage Paul speaks of the characteristics of his life and ministry. These are his credentials, the example he has set forth by his life.

Paul was second to none as an apostle; in fact, he was the chief apostle. He endured all kinds of afflictions, persecutions, and perils in his faithful service to the Lord. He wants us to examine his badge of authority for the office of apostle. "Look at my doctrine, my manner of life, my purpose, my faith, my longsuffering, my love, my patience."

These are the things by which we are to judge ourselves and others—by fruit, not by words alone. The life of the apostle Paul was faithful, and it was fruitful. Christians' lives, especially that of ministers of the gospel, are evidenced by the fruit produced in their lives.

FOLLOW PAUL'S EXAMPLE

Paul is telling us two things in this passage.

First: "Look at my manner of life, my doctrine, my purpose. Look at my faith and longsuffering.

Persecutions came, and I had to endure them, but the Lord delivered me out of them all."

In other scriptures he says: "Follow me as I follow Christ. Look at my life as an example for you to imitate. Look at how I endured the persecutions, how I was full of faith, longsuffering, charity, and patience. Take note of that, and re¬member everything I have taught you."

Second: "Continue in the things you have learned. Evil men and seducers are going to wax worse and worse. They are going to deceive and be deceived. But continue in what you've learned. Continue in what I've taught you and be assured that it will deliver you from perilous times."

We know Paul is talking about perilous times because he says so. "This know also, that in the last days perilous times shall come" (2 Tim. 3:1). We are experiencing these perilous times now.

Take a look around you. There is crime (murder, robbery, rape), economic problems (inflation, unemployment, depression, starvation), in natural disasters (floods, earthquakes, droughts). There is an increase in almost everything harmful and destructive.

This is not God's best. He never intended for the earth and humanity to suffer such things.

In Romans 8:22 Paul says the whole earth, all of creation, is groaning and travailing until it is set free— free from sin. The earth was never designed to stagger under the effects of sin. The sin nature was never God's intended purpose and plan for mankind. When this world is finally freed from the bonds and effects of sin, the millennial reign will be ushered in, and there will be a tremendous change! (See Rev. 20:1–6.)

Paul says here that if you will continue in the things you have learned, be assured of them, and know of whom you have learned them, you can thrive in perilous times.

FEAR NOT

Some people blame God for the way things are. They say, "If God would just do something...." God did something. He sent Jesus—His Word. The Bible says, "He sent his word, and healed them, and delivered them from their destructions" (Ps. 107:20).

Some theologians say this refers only to spiritual healing and deliverance. But the stripes that Jesus bore on His back guaranteed our physical as well as our spiritual healing. The Bible is full of scriptures that tell us to be sound—spirit, soul, and body. The triune being, the whole man, should be prosperous. God wants your spirit (the real you) to be born again. He wants your mind (your soulish part) to be renewed. He wants your body to be healthy as His divine life operates through you.

Paul says we can live victoriously in perilous times. Even though such times are coming, we can stand firmly against them. When the enemy comes in like a flood, we can know that a standard has been raised against him. (Isa. 59:19.)

As a believer, you are a part of that standard. You are a part of the body of Christ, and Satan cannot overcome *you*. The Word of God in the hands of a believer is a standard against which Satan cannot succeed. Jesus said, "Upon this rock I will build my church; and the gates of hell shall not prevail against it" (Matt. 16:18). Satan cannot prevail against the body of Christ or any believer who knows how to wield the Word of God.

WHATSOEVER YOU SOW

What did Paul teach the New Testament churches he raised up?

In Galatians 6:7 he said, "Be not deceived." This refers to the first instruction of Jesus we read from Matthew 24, "Take heed that no man deceive you" (v. 4).

Paul told the Galatians that they had been deceived. They had fallen away from the Word he had taught them and had turned back to the bondage of Jewish law. So he wrote: "O foolish Galatians, who hath bewitched you, that ye should not obey the truth" (Gal. 3:1).

He dealt strongly with them in one particular area: "But though we, or an angel from heaven, preach any other gospel unto you than that which we have preached unto you, let him be accursed" (Gal. 1:8).

The problem with many Christians is they are not continuing in what they have learned. They are listening to the traditions and opinions of men rather than the Word of God.

SOWING AND REAPING

Be not deceived; God is not mocked: for whatsoever a man soweth, that shall he also reap. For he that soweth to his flesh shall of the flesh reap corruption; but he that soweth to the Spirit shall of the Spirit reap life everlasting. And let us not be weary in well doing; for in due season we shall reap, if we faint not. As we have therefore opportunity, let us do good unto all men, especially unto them who are of the household of faith.

Galatians 6:7–10

One way that Satan oppresses people and keeps them in bondage is through financial problems. People who are in financial poverty are bound; but God never intended for man to be bound in any way by Satan.

In these verses from Galatians, Paul speaks about a principle in life which has a direct bearing upon freedom from bondage. He is teaching the people in Galatia that those who sow in the realm of the Spirit will of the Spirit reap everlasting life. Now everlasting, or eternal, life does not begin when you get to heaven. It is for today—here and now—as much as for our future life in heaven.

Paul is telling us how to operate in that Word for today. He is saying, "Don't be deceived. God is not mocked. Whatever a person sows, that is what he is going to reap. Don't get tired of doing good, because if you continue to sow, in due time you will reap. Do good to people every chance you get, especially to other believers."

If you are struggling financially, don't hold onto the little you have and ignore those around you who are in need. The Bible plainly teaches that to receive we must give. To reap, we must sow.

Proverbs 11:24 says, "There is that scattereth, and

yet increaseth; and there is that withholdeth more than is meet, but it tendeth to poverty."

Jesus said, "Give, and it shall be given unto you; good measure, pressed down, and shaken together, and running over, shall men give into your bosom. For with the same measure that ye mete withal it shall be measured to you again" (Luke 6:38).

You might say, "Yes, I know the principle of sowing and reaping, of giving and receiving. I've heard that many times, and I've been giving. But it doesn't seem to be working."

Don't be deceived by what you see.

FAINT NOT

If you expect the principle of sowing and reaping (or any principle of the Bible) to work for you, you must continue in it. Whatever you sow will come back to you. Don't be weary in well doing. In due season you will reap, if you don't faint or give up.

This is what Paul was saying in 2 Timothy 3:14

when he said continue in the things you have learned.
Now is not the time to quit. Now is the time to continue
in the things you have learned.

DON'T QUIT

The apostle Paul wrote:

Of the Jews five times received I forty stripes
save one. Thrice was I beaten with rods, once
was I stoned, thrice I suffered shipwreck, a
night and a day I have been in the deep; In
journeyings often, in perils of waters, in perils
of robbers, in perils by mine own countrymen,
in perils by the heathen, in perils in the city, in
perils in the wilderness, in perils in the sea, in
perils among false brethren; In weariness and
painfulness, in watchings often, in hunger and
thirst, in fastings often, in cold and nakedness.
Beside those things that are without, that
which cometh upon me daily, the care of all
the churches.

2 Corinthians 11:24–28

Perils, afflictions, persecutions—the apostle Paul suffered them all. He was shipwrecked, stoned, imprisoned, criticized, hounded, and opposed. Besides that, he carried the care of all the churches he had begun. It was his duty and responsibility to keep them in line. Some of his best friends forsook him. (See 2 Tim. 4:10–11.) The man actually hurt inside because of the care of these people and because of the rejection he experienced. Yet he remained strong in the faith.

In *Philippians 3:13–14* he wrote:

Brethren, I count not myself to have apprehended: but this one thing I do, forgetting those things which are behind, and reaching forth unto those things which are before, I press toward the mark.

Here is the key to Paul's success: Besides being a man of faith and God's chosen vessel, *he simply refused to quit*. He believed so much in what he was doing that he continued in the things he had learned. That is *your* key to succeed and thrive in perilous times: *Don't quit!*

5

Know the Word

From a child thou hast known the holy
scriptures, which are able to make thee wise
unto salvation through faith which is in Christ
Jesus.

2 Timothy 3:15

The final thing Paul tells us about how to live in
perilous times is *know the Scriptures, which will make
us wise.*

You may say, "I don't need wisdom. I need health,
money, and a good job. I need all kinds of things, but
wisdom isn't one of them."

If you had wisdom, you could acquire all those
other things. Wisdom is the knowledge of God. God
knows what is going to happen in the future. He can
protect you from the economy and guide you in your
investments

THE ISSUES OF LIFE

In *Proverbs 4:20–23* God says several things about wisdom:

> My son, attend to my words; incline thine ear unto my sayings. Let them not depart from thine eyes; keep them in the midst of thine heart. For they are life unto those that find them, and health to all their flesh. Keep thy heart with all diligence; for out of it are the issues of life.

God is telling us how to succeed in this life. Most people think that the life they are longing for is out ahead of them, and if they could just lay hold on it, everything would be all right. But no matter how hard they run, life always seems to escape them, to outdistance them. How wrong they are!

Life is not out ahead of you; it is within you. God's Word says that life proceeds out of your heart. "Keep your heart with all diligence; for out of it proceed the issues [or forces] of life." When we are born again, the life of God is placed inside us.

You are not trying to *get* life; you already *have* it.

LIFE AND HEALTH

These verses in Proverbs tell us to tend to God's Word. According to this passage, the first two products of God's Word are life and health.

Know the Scriptures, and they will make you wise. Then that wisdom will produce for you life and health. But that's not all.

THE KNOWLEDGE OF GOD

In *Proverbs 2:1–5* God says something else about how to live in success and abundance:

My son, if thou wilt receive my words, and hide my commandments with thee; so that thou incline thine ear unto wisdom, and apply thine heart to understanding; Yea, if thou criest after knowledge, and liftest up thy voice for understanding; if thou seekest her as silver, and searchest for her as for hid treasures; then shalt thou understand the fear of the Lord, and find the knowledge of God.

What more could anyone need to thrive in perilous times than the knowledge of God? The Bible says here that if you will seek after God's Word, or wisdom, as silver and search for her as for hidden treasures, you will understand the fear of the Lord. This fear does not refer to a spirit of fear, but to the power, holiness, and awesomeness of God. It does not imply fright, but reverence.

Every television news broadcast is telling you how far prices are going up, how far your income is going down, how fearful it is to purchase a house, how bad the weather is going to be, and how few minutes are left on the doomsday clock.

What are you going to do when that danger, fear, dread, and apprehension comes against you? Paul said know the Scriptures, and they would make you wise. Wisdom—the knowledge of God—will help you live victoriously in these dangerous and perilous times.

THE WISDOM OF GOD

For the Lord giveth wisdom: out of his mouth
cometh knowledge and understanding.

Proverbs 2:6

If you want true wisdom, you must get it from
God. Out of God's mouth comes His Word, which is
why Paul said to know the Scriptures and you would be
wise. You will be unaffected by perilous times because
you will know how to deal with them.

Psalm 91:10 says, "There shall no evil befall thee,
neither shall any plague come nigh thy dwelling."
No danger can upset you because God's Word will
deliver you from the noisome pestilence. No raging
epidemic, plague, or evil shall befall you. If you have
the knowledge and wisdom of God, you will dwell in
the secret place of the Most High. (v. 1.)

Proverbs 2:7 says, "He layeth up sound wisdom for
the righteous: he is a buckler to them that walk uprightly."
Because you are the righteous, sound wisdom is laid up
for *you*. As you walk uprightly, according to the Word,

God will be a buckler, or shield, to *you*.

> He keepeth the paths of judgment, and
> preserveth the way of his saints.
>
> *Proverbs 2:8*

Because you are one of God's saints, God will
preserve your way. Think about this. Meditate on it
and confess it until it gets down into your spirit, until
you know it is for you: *"God will preserve my way!"*

If you will lay up God's Word, seek after His
wisdom, keep the paths of judgment, and walk uprightly,
God will preserve (guard, protect) your way. You will
know the Scriptures, and they will make you wise.

GOD'S UNDERSTANDING

> Then shalt thou understand righteousness, and
> judgment, and equity; yea, every good path.
>
> *Proverbs 2:9*

If you have the knowledge and wisdom of God, you
can live above the calamities that come upon the earth.

Proverbs 2:11 says, "Discretion shall preserve thee." If you want to be preserved, then know wisdom—know God's Word. That wisdom will produce discretion (the ability to make good, responsible, correct decisions); and that discretion will preserve you.

"Understanding shall keep thee." It shall keep you from trouble, turmoil, poverty, sickness, disease—every kind of destructive force that Satan can send against you.

When you have a knowledge and understanding of God, you will know how to handle *every* situation—*every* test, trial, and problem that comes your way—and how to apply the Word of God. That is why Paul said if you will know the Scriptures, they will make you wise. Being wise is having the knowledge of God. God is unaffected by perilous times, and you are made in His image and likeness. You have His life, His faith, His Word.

WALK THROUGH THE PROBLEMS

We believers should never be affected by perilous times. Problems are going to come. But we have the knowledge, wisdom, understanding, and discretion of

God to walk through those problems and overcome them. Being spiritual does not mean you will have fewer problems. But you will be able to go through those problems faster, because you face them with the Word.

SEEK AFTER WISDOM

> Happy is the man that findeth wisdom, and the
> man that getteth understanding.
>
> *Proverbs 3:13*

This is one of my favorite Scripture verses. When I first read it, I said, "Thank You, Lord. You wrote that for me. I receive it for my own. That is my scripture and I stand on it."

Then God said, "Son, you can take that scripture and apply it to yourself. But read it carefully and meditate on it. You'll see something else." So I read it, meditated on it, and studied it until I saw what God wanted me to see. That verse says, "Happy is the man that *findeth* wisdom, and...*getteth* understanding."

Wisdom and understanding will not fall on you like

74

apples off a tree. You have to search for wisdom, seek and desire it with all your heart, if you are to have it.

When you have found it, you will have the results of it—the knowledge of God. Wisdom helps you to thrive in perilous times. Know the Scriptures, and they will make you wise.

RESULTS OF WISDOM

Now I want *you* to see what wisdom and understanding will do for you:

> Happy is the man that findeth wisdom, and the man that getteth understanding. For the merchandise of it is better than the merchandise of silver, and the gain thereof than fine gold. She is more precious than rubies: and all the things thou canst desire are not to be compared unto her. Length of days is in her right hand; and in her left hand riches and honour.
>
> *Proverbs 3:13-16*

When we seek after and find wisdom, the

merchandise of it (what it will produce) is better than silver and gold. It is more precious than rubies. Besides that, with wisdom there will be length of days, or long life; and to have long life, you must have good health.

Seek wisdom instead of riches, and you will have riches and honor too. Don't struggle after riches and honor. Don't worry about your reputation. Just do what God has told you: Seek after the wisdom and understanding of God; the riches and honor will come.

YOU SHALL NOT BE AFRAID

Her [wisdom's] ways are ways of pleasantness, and all her paths are peace. She is a tree of life to them that lay hold upon her: and happy is every one that retaineth her. The Lord by wisdom hath founded the earth; by understanding hath he established the heavens. By his knowledge the depths are broken up, and the clouds drop down the dew. My son, let not them [God's words] depart from thine eyes: keep sound wisdom and discretion: So

shall they be life unto thy soul, and grace to
thy neck.

Proverbs 3:17–22

When you find God's wisdom, you will have life
in your soul. You will have grace and peace.

Verse 23 says, "Then shalt thou walk in thy way
safely, and thy foot shall not stumble." This means
every step you take and every decision you make will
be right. You will neither stumble nor fall. You need not
be afraid of failing, because wisdom will guide you.

"When thou liest down, thou shalt not be afraid:
yea, thou shalt lie down, and thy sleep shall be sweet"
(v. 24). You won't have to worry about any of the
problems or situations you face. When you lie down,
your sleep will be sweet.

"Be not afraid of sudden fear, neither of the
desolation of the wicked, when it cometh" (v. 25).
Don't be afraid of sudden impending danger. Don't be
afraid if you hear about some crop failure or shortage.
God is your Source. His wisdom and His Word will

put you over.

"For the Lord shall be thy confidence, and shall keep thy foot from being taken" (v. 26). You will be unconcerned about things to come because God's Word will be your confidence. You will know that, come what may, your feet will not be taken; you will not be overcome.

IMPORTANCE OF WISDOM

Knowing the Scriptures will make one wise. How important wisdom is! *Proverbs 4:6–7* says of wisdom:

> Forsake her not, and she shall preserve thee: love her, and she shall keep thee. Wisdom is the principal thing; therefore get wisdom: and with all thy getting get understanding.

Let me emphasize this phrase: "Wisdom is the principal thing." These words are so strong, so important to every Christian.

The Scriptures—God's wisdom—will keep you and protect you. You won't be afraid of sudden fear. You will lie down at night and not be afraid; your sleep will be sweet. You will walk in safety; your feet will not stumble. Your life will be great. The Word of God will keep you in all your ways.

> Exalt her [wisdom], and she shall promote thee: she shall bring thee to honour, when thou dost embrace her. She shall give to thine head an ornament of grace: a crown of glory shall she deliver to thee.
>
> *Proverbs 4:8,9*

Exalt (value highly) wisdom and it will promote you. You don't have to seek after promotion of riches. "The *love* of money is the root of all evil" (1 Tim. 6:10). When people seek after money and such things, they err from the faith and pierce themselves through with many sorrows. (vv. 9–10.)

> Hear, O my son, and receive my sayings; and the years of thy life shall be many. I have taught thee in the way of wisdom; I have led thee in right paths. When thou goest, thy steps shall not be straitened; and when thou

runnest, thou shalt not stumble. Take fast hold
of instruction; let her not go: keep her; for she
is thy life.

Proverbs 4:10–13

That is powerful. Wisdom is the principal thing.
Above all things, get wisdom and get understanding.
The importance of wisdom cannot be overstated,
because wisdom produces everything you need for life.

WISDOM SHALL KEEP THEE

God's Word says wisdom will keep you during
perilous times. Suppose you hear a television news
broadcast that some calamity is coming.

In the spring, the broadcasters in my part of the
country start warning that the "tornado season" is upon
us. They broadcast their negative reports out into the
atmosphere. To combat that, we have to release our
positive confessions. We boldly announce: "No evil
shall befall us, and no plague shall come near our
dwelling." We release our faith in the Word of God,

and that faith causes fear to depart.

Fear, if permitted to remain unchallenged, will open the door to all kinds of destruction and calamity. Fear of sickness or disease will actually produce those symptoms. Many people have opened themselves to Satan's attacks this way. Then they say, "I guess it's just my fate in life."

According to the Bible, if you are a child of God, your "fate" is financial prosperity, a healthy body, and a prosperous soul. *Third John 2* says so:

> Beloved, I. wish above *all* things that thou mayest *prosper* and *be in health*, even as thy soul prospereth.

That is God's will for you, if you avail yourself of it by knowing the Word of God, which produces wisdom and understanding. You take that wisdom and apply it to your situation. You speak the Word in faith and it goes forth to produce the thing which you have spoken.

You *can* thrive in perilous times…

…if you don't allow yourself to be deceived.

...if you don't allow yourself to be troubled.

...if you continue in the things you have learned.

...if you know the Word of God.

Prayer of Salvation

God loves you—no matter who you are, no matter what your past. God loves you so much that He gave His one and only begotten Son for you. The Bible tells us that "whoever believes in him shall not perish but have eternal life" (John 3:16 NIV). Jesus laid down His life and rose again so that we could spend eternity with Him in heaven and experience His absolute best on earth. If you would like to receive Jesus into your life, say the following prayer out loud and mean it from your heart.

Heavenly Father, I come to You admitting that I am a sinner. Right now, I choose to turn away from sin, and I ask You to cleanse me of all unrighteousness. I believe that Your Son, Jesus, died on the cross to take away my sins. I also believe that He rose again from the dead so that I might be forgiven of my sins and made righteous through faith in Him. I call upon the name of Jesus Christ to be the Savior and Lord of my life. Jesus, I choose to follow You and ask that You fill me with the power of the Holy Spirit. I declare that right now I am a child of God. I am free from sin and full of the righteousness of God. I am saved in Jesus' name. Amen.

If you prayed this prayer to receive Jesus Christ as your Savior for the first time, please contact us on the web at **www.harrisonhouse.com** to receive a free book.

Or you may write to us at
Harrison House
P.O. Box 35035
Tulsa, Oklahoma 74153

About the Author

In 1979 God spoke to Happy Caldwell to build a spiritual production center in Little Rock, in order to take the good news of Jesus Christ to the city, state, nation and world. Happy and his wife Jeanne founded Agape Church, a strong spirit-filled body of believers. Through his deep sensitivity to the Spirit of God, and his anointed teaching, the lost are being saved, the sick healed, and thousands are being blessed.

In 1988 Happy and Jeanne answered a direct call from the Lord to take His message beyond Central Arkansas. They founded VTN--the Victory Television Network. This network of 3 full-power TV stations is carried on over 200 cable systems and is bringing the Gospel into more than 1.2 million households. Through his own daily program, Arkansas Alive, Happy presents the Word in profound simplicity, making the character of God a revelation to those who hear.

Also desiring to see spiritual excellence in education, the ministry of Agape has grown to include an elementary academy, a school of world evangelism, and Agape College which offers both diploma and degree programs.

Happy's ministry is known for instilling Christian

principles in strategic leadership. He was honored for this in 2005 with an invitation to participate in the US Army War College Strategic Leader Staff Ride.

He is a recipient of the Peter J. Daniels Caleb Encourager Award, which has been bestowed upon such notable names as Norman Vincent Peale, Nelson Mandela, and Dr. Oral Roberts. He has also been recognized by the Arkansas Martin Luther King Jr. Commission with The Salute to Greatness Community Service Award.

Happy Caldwell continues to travel worldwide delivering the life-changing message of Jesus Christ. He has recorded several albums with his wife, Jeanne, and has written several books including Saving Our Cities, No More Limits, and An Expected End.

You may contact Happy Caldwell
by writing to:
Agape Church, Inc.
P. O. Box 22007
Little Rock, AR 72221-2007
www.agape-church.org

Please include your prayer requests
and comments when you write.

The Harrison House Vision

Proclaiming the truth and the power
Of the Gospel of Jesus Christ
With excellence;
Challenging Christians to
Live victoriously,
Grow spiritually,
Know God intimately.